THE ARCHAEOLOGICAL EXPLORATIONS OF ARUNACHAL PRADESH

THE BRIEF HISTORY OF EXPLORATIONS

ISHWAR SINGH

I am dedicating this book to my parents Sardar Pal Singh and Sardarni Amarjit Kaur who brought me into this beautiful world and made me capable of being what I am today.

Contents

Foreword

The author of this book is my younger brother. He has very interest in book writing. The author has the potential to write the non fictional and academic books. Few years ago, i had advised him to write books for the future generations so that they could know about their society and culture. At last i am leaving this discussion with a quote written by Ishwar Singh.

"An Archeological Site is just like a mirror which reflects about the ancient and medieval civilization ."

Ishwar Singh

Preface

Dear Readers

It gives me great pleasure to present before you the collection of my notes in the form of a book. In this book, I have tried to use very simple language, quality photographs regarding situation of our archeological excavations.

As you read the title of this book which is 'The Archaeological Excavations of Arunachal Pradesh' you can understand the motive of this book. This book talks about the present situation of our archeological Sites.

I have tried to do research on our precious archeological sites so that we can understand the medieval period and being engaged with our traditional culture. I just want to explore the some important archeological sites of Arunachal Pradesh so that our future generations could know about importance of it.

I have tried to express my views in very short words and just briefly explain the various sites. I think you will enjoy this book and engage

yourself in a thorough reading.

Thank you

Acknowledgements

I am over helmed in all humbleness and gratefulness to acknowledge my depth to all those who have helped me to put these ideas, well above the level of simplicity and into something concrete.

I would like to express my special thanks of gratitude to my professor who gave me the golden opportunity to do this wonderful project on the 'The Archaeological Explorations of Arunachal Pradesh', which also helped me in doing a lot of Research and i came to know about so many new things. I am really thankful to them.

Any attempt at any level can 't be satisfactorily completed without the support and guidance of MY parents and friends.

I would like to thank my parents who helped me a lot in gathering different information, collecting data and guiding me from time to time in making this project, despite of their busy schedules, they gave me different ideas in

making this project unique.

Prologue

India is a country of huge cultural diversities. This diversity has its roots in the ancient and medieval period of the history. In present day life, every one is playing his role according to the role assingned by the nature. I have very much interest to explore various cultural aspects of our indian society. So an idea came in my mind to explore our archaeological sites in various states. In this book i am focusing on the archaeological situations of Arunachal Pradesh. I am writing this book for our younger generations so that when they will read this book, they must understand the civilisation of our forefathers.

CHAPTER ONE

Introduction

An archaeological site is a place (or group of physical sites) in which evidence of past activity is preserved (either prehistoric or historic or contemporary), and which has been, or may be, investigated using the discipline of archaeology and represents a part of the archaeological record. Sites may range from those with few or no remains visible above ground, to buildings and other structures still in use.

Arunachal Pradesh is a state in Northeastern India. It was formed from the erstwhile North-East FrontierAgency (NEFA) region, and became a state on 20 February 1987.

It borders the states of Assam and Nagaland to the south. It shares international borders with Bhutan in the west, Myanmar in the east, and a disputed border with China in the north at the McMahon Line.

Itanagar is the state capital of Arunachal Pradesh. Arunachal Pradesh is the largest of the Seven Sister States of Northeast India by area. Arunachal Pradesh shares a 1,129 km border with China's Tibet Autonomous Region.[1]

Refrences

....

1. "Mapping India and China's disputed borders". Al Jazeera. 10 September 2020. Retrieved 27 January 2021.

CHAPTER TWO

Dirang Dzong

Dirang Dzong or Dirang fort was built in the 17th century to protect Bomdila from the neighbouring states. The fort was used as a jail and during the world war period. It is located atop a hill and comprises of four storied fortified stone slabs that are supported by wooden logs. The entrance wooden gate is decorated with local architectural designs and is definitely an eye catcher. The architecture of these houses is worth appreciating.[1]

Dirang Dzong, which is an innate territory, is on the shores of Dirang River. The design of the ancestral state is dazzling. A portion of the houses are more than 500 years of age. The houses were worked to manage the antagonistic climate in the area. The establishment of these houses is of stone and the dividers and rooftop are worked of wood. Dzong, as the fortification is alluded to involves this settlement and it rouses you with its engineering, which is an impact of Buddhist kingdoms. Despite the fact that the stronghold is presently in ruins, the vestiges are verification of design greatness of the long time past days. Perspectives from Dirang Dzong are astounding.[2]

Dirang Dzong Fort[Source: www.hellotravel.com]

Refrences

....

1. www.incredibleindia.org
2. www.hellotravel.com

CHAPTER THREE

Taklung Dzang

The monastery was founded in 1180 CE by Taklung Thangpa Tashi Pal (1142–1210), on a site previously inhabited by a famous Kadampa lama, Potowa Rinchen Sel, who was a disciple of Dromton , Atisha's chief disciple. It is the main seat of the Taklung Kagyu, one of the four chief schools of the Kagyu sect.[1]

Through the efforts of Taklung Thangpa Tashi Pal, and his immediate successors, the number of monks eventually increased to 7,000. The main temple known as the Tsuklakhang (the Jokhang of Taklung) was completed in 1228.

"The *sTag-lung-pa* Lama [about the end of the 12th century] exemplifies the disciplined and pious existence of the founder of a great monastery. The *Blue Annals* (pp. 610-20) describes the simple austerity of his life, which was a continual process of silent meditation, preaching, ceremonies and rites. No wine or meat was allowed in his monastery, and no woman might enter his house. He never went for a walk beyond the limits of his monastery, and he never failed to attend to the rites and teachings given by his own Lama *Phag-mo-gru* (1110-1170 CE). His advice was constantly sought, and he was frequently called upon to mediate in the disputes of his contemporaries."[2]

Taklung Dzong[Source: ignca.gov.in]

Taklung Dzong[Source: ignca.gov.in]

Refrences

1. Taklung Kagyu
2. Snellgrove & Richardson (1968), p. 150.

CHAPTER FOUR

Naksaparbat

Naksaparbat is an archeological site with ruins of a medieval settlement located in the foothills of East Kameng district. As per archaeological reports, the ruins can be dated to 14th-15th century built by kings of the Chutia kingdom. During the excavation carried out by the Archaeological Department, several stone carvings were observed in the stone pillars. These were actually mason marks made on stone plinth of wooden houses.

Similar mason marks have been found in archaeological sites of Sadiya as well. For example, in the Tamreswari temple, Bura-buri Than, Padum pukhuri, etc. Besides these, sites like Malini Than, Buroi hill fort also contains such marks which points to the fact that all these structures were built by the same people. This has been acknowledged by historians like Kanaklal Barua and Maheswar Neog too.

The stone marks found in the Tamreswari temple were present in the stone foundation of the brick wall, which was constructed by the Chutia king Muktadharmanarayana in 1442. This fact proves that all these structures including Nakshaparbat were build by Chutia kings in that same era.[1]

Ruins at Naksa Parbat [Source: thenamorahcamp.home.blog]

Close up of a pillar [Source: thenamorahcamp.home.blog]

Refrences

....

1. www.quora.com

CHAPTER FIVE

Itafort

Ita Fort in Itanagar town, is one of the most important historical sites in the state of Arunachal Pradesh, India. The name literally means "Fort of bricks"(brick being called "Ita" in the Assamese language). The Ita Fort at Arunachal Pradesh was built as early as the 14th or the 15th century.

The fort has an irregular shape, built mainly with bricks dating back to the 14th-15th Century. The total brickwork is of 16,200 cubic metre

lengths which was probably built by kings of the Chutiya kingdom which ruled the region during that time. The fort has three different entrances at three different sides, which are western, the eastern and the southern sides.[1]

Ruins of Itafort[Source: arunachaltimes.in]

Ruins of Itafort[Source: AshLin]

Ruins of Itafort[Source: AshLin]

Refrences

....

1. www.papumpare.nic.in

CHAPTER SIX

Malinithan

Malinithan is an archaeological site which consists of ruins of a Hindu temple of the early medieval period on the northern bank of the Brahmaputra River in the Indian state of Arunachal Pradesh.

The archaeological excavations revealed a very well designed and carved plinth of a temple, of 8 feet (2.4 m) height, sculptures of deities and animals, designs of flowers, damaged columns and panels. Four sculptures of lions on two

elephants were found at the four corners of the ruins of the temple.

Among the sculptures found at Malinthan, five notable ones carved out of granite stone are of Indra riding his mount Airavata, Kartikeya riding a peacock, Surya (Sun) riding a chariot, and Ganesha mounted over a mouse, and a large Nandi bull.[1]

As per the mythology constructed, when Krishna wanted to marry Rukmini, the daughter of King Bhishmaka of Vidarbha, he abducted her prior to her wedding with Shishupala. Krishna and Rukmini then travelled from Bhishmakanagar to Dwarka, stopping at Malinithan on the way over, where they were guests of Shiva and Durga, who were doing penance. Parvati, Shiva's consort, warmly welcoming her guests, presented them with garlands made of flowers plucked from her orchard.[2]

Ruins of Malinithan Temple [Source: www.assam.com]

Refrences

1. Shin, Jae-Eun (2020). "Descending from demons, ascending to kshatriyas: Genealogical claims and political process in pre-modern Northeast India, The Chutiyas and the Dimasas". The Indian Economic and Social History Review.
2. Sali, M. L. (1 January 1998). India-China Border Dispute: A Case Study of the Eastern Sector. APH Publishing.

CHAPTER SEVEN

Gorcham Chortan

Gorcham Chortan is situated at Zemithang, 92 km away from Tawang, one of the largest Buddhist stupas in Asia with a plinth area of 186 feet and a height of 100 feet. The massive religious structure exhibits a unique monastic architecture with stone and mud having a Tri-Ratha base constructed by Lama Prathar during the 17th century AD which took 12years to complete.

The Chorten looks the same from all the four sides & the top view, which can seen from the mountains around is even majestic. It is believed that the Stupa has a vast repository of ancient Tibetian texts, literature & other artifacts. The Stupa is opened very 12 years wherein the books & texts are revisited by the lamas. The opening of the Stupa is celebrated with great fanfare & a lot of Buddhist people visit this location during that time of the year & the festivities continue during the entire time (approx 10 days) when the Stupa is open. After the celebrations the stupa is permanently closed with brick & cement for the next 12 years (a small door is made in between the eyes on the top). There are three Stupas of this kind, one in Nepal, one in Bhutan & this one. His Holiness 14th Dalai Lama entered India from Tibet in 1959 from a place called Khinzemane (10 km from Zimithang) & believed to have rested here.[1]

Gorcham Chortan [Source: tawang.nic.in]

Refrences

1. www.tripadvisor.in

CHAPTER EIGHT

Thembang Dzong

The Thembang Village/Dzong is a fortified traditional Monpa village situated in the Dirang circle of West Kameng district at an altitude of 2172 Mtr above MSL, having 39 households with 178 populations (2014) covering an area of 3.2 acres of land belonging to C18AD. The entire village is bounded by a fort with 2 (two) gates made of stones, wood, and mud mortar. The residential houses are of the old settlement pattern having Buddhist architect and the lifestyle of people viz. Dirkhipas also bears testimony of their past. There is a historical

account about the Dzong in the book Garep written by Norbu Tashi in 1165 AD. The two gates were rebuilt in 2007, The UNESCO has enlisted the Thembang Dzong in the tentative list of World Heritage Sites under the living Monument heritage category in 2015 along with 55 other sites in India, which also included the Apatani Valley- under the Cultural Landscapes heritage category. [1]

A Site at Thembang Village [Source: ai.stanford.edu]

Refrences

....

1. www.arunachal.kammarkia.com

Conclusion

We have studied the brief history about various archaeological sites like Dirang Dzong, Taklung Dzang, Naksaparbat, Itafort, Malinithan, Gorcham Chortan and Thembang Dzong. Out of which Taklung Dzang, Itafort and Malinithan have very little remains left, which required further protection and other arrangements by the government for the betterment of such sites.

9 798886 670905

Printed by Libri Plureos GmbH in Hamburg, Germany